# THE
# LOVE DIET

**LEIGH KELLIS**

**BALBOA.**PRESS
A DIVISION OF HAY HOUSE

Balboa Press books may be ordered through booksellers or by contacting:

Balboa Press
A Division of Hay House
1663 Liberty Drive
Bloomington, IN 47403
www.balboapress.com
844-682-1282

Print information available on the last page.

ISBN: 978-1-9822-5356-1 (sc)
ISBN: 978-1-9822-5357-8 (e)

Balboa Press rev. date: 02/22/2021

# CONTENTS

# PREFACE

I am a fake. I wrote a book called *Women Who Need Donuts* about eating donuts, making a business out of love, and allowing oneself to eat in pleasure and joy. Honor your cravings! Live! Indulge! Allow! It's all good!

And I'm full of shit. I don't do any of those things.

The past three years have been a doozy. After my dad died, I continued on a downward spiral of poor health, weight gain, and struggle. I couldn't figure out the connection. I cut out gluten, dairy, sugar, wine, life, everything. I went on pleasure lockdown because I was so miserable in my body.

After three years, I found that food didn't cure me entirely. Restricting didn't cure me. Restricting spiraled out of control. I was unable to fix myself and get a grip and cope with the pain I didn't realize had always been in my heart. Today, I was talking to my therapist and confessed that I have an eating disorder.

I said, "Here I am, the Donut Queen, and I don't even eat my own donuts. I can't."

I can't eat them because of food fear. I literally panic at the thought of a donut because I have been tiptoeing around my discomfort in my body for these three years, and the pain has been too raw. I didn't even know what the exposed raw nerve was, but it's insecurity, unworthiness, and fear. It's fear of being human, having an "imperfect body," not being loved, not feeling beautiful. I needed self-love. I needed soothing. Coping. Soul medicine.

I've been frantically looking for this relief through my diet. I thought cutting out gluten and sugar would save me, heal me, fix me, anesthetize the pain. It didn't work.

I'll tell you what worked. It was the opposite of pleasure lockdown.

This is the love diet.

# INTRODUCTION

I wrote a book called *Women Who Need Donuts*. I read through it now, and I am amazed at the personal wisdom I had then. I believed my own words then. I do believe them now, but something got in the way: fear, doubt, and a total bottoming out of belief in myself.

I don't know why this happened, but it's become clear that messages and pain resurface until you get the lesson. I thought I had figured it all out; I had not. The deep sense of unworthiness was hiding beneath the surface. The beast had not been cured. The terror of not being loveable as is was sitting in me, *not* healed.

Right when I published that book, my dad died. I acknowledged at that time that losing a father leaves a void—a void that requires an opportunity to turn toward something else to replace the sense of security in the world that dads are designed to provide. The only option to replace that security, I found, is God.

I guess the bottoming out was the realization that my faith was rocky at best. I didn't believe in a God who was on my side. I didn't believe in life that can be really magical and beautiful. I didn't believe that things actually work out. Most importantly, I didn't believe in the God in myself that is my true source of security, faith, hope, and magic. This is where I got derailed. I had to go through the fire of feeling like total shit and losing all hope in life and myself to see this emptiness clearly, then dig myself out of the hole of self-doubt and restriction to crawl across broken glass back to a sense of belief in myself, in God, in life.

This is the love diet.

The love diet is a steady diet of love, faith, listening to your intuition, and trusting yourself, your cravings, your choices, your capabilities, and your ability to love. And it's eating whatever the fuck you want.

# THE STORY

I N HIGH SCHOOL, I was normal. I was healthy. I ate food and had a life. I didn't feel horribly insecure. I had friends and didn't have a traumatizing high school experience like a lot of people did. Senior year, though, I remember everybody started talking about the oat bran diet. It was 1993. Eat oat bran! Just sprinkle it on everything! It's gross but it fills you up, slims you down, and who doesn't want to slim down? Nobody, I guess?

*Everyone needs to be better* was how I interpreted this craze. So I absorbed this new mentality as *it's time to be fixed, something must need to be fixed!* That's where it started. I connected the food piece to becoming more beautiful, more acceptable, more loveable. And everything went to shit from there.

I went to college and sunk into despair. I went two hours north to my state college. I didn't want to go to this college; I wanted to get the hell out of Maine and see the world. I wanted California, somewhere warm, somewhere tropical and exotic. But I shipped off to central Maine and froze to death and drank too much alcohol and lost my virginity. I started binge-eating. Every day, I'd try to be good, stay in the lines, eat well, power walk, and be normal. I didn't feel normal; I felt like a total mess. Everybody was hooking up, and this made my body self-consciousness go through the roof.

I'd go through the motions by day, dragging myself to class, and then sit in my dorm room at night desperate for comfort and soothing due to being away from home and feeling untethered. I'd eat, and then I'd tell myself to stop. Then I couldn't. I'd binge from a place of being totally off the rails, sad, and out of control. It was like an inner beast I couldn't contain. It was an appetite with a depth with no bottom, and I hated myself.

I repeated this daily, and it snowballed. It was despair. It was a cry for help to myself, and I hid it from others because I was so ashamed. It was my little secret of sadness and self-hatred. I lived in a small, isolated world of the cycle of self-abuse. It was sad. It was protection. It was coping with life in the most perverted way, self-soothing through self-punishment.

Ugh, it was so painful. I didn't trust myself with food, and I couldn't be at peace with myself. I was a sad little girl just wanting comfort. That was who she was. And twenty-five years later, that little girl resurfaced.

This time is different, though. I can see her. I can feel the pain, and I love her. Miraculously, I found my way out of the cage. I'm still crawling out now, as I write, but there is hope now. I see it with love. The love diet. Love that little hungry girl. She wanted and wants love and cookies and hugs and security and comfort. That's all she wants. It's a beautiful compulsion, the compulsion to want love and a beautiful life. I thought she was a hungry, crazy beast. Now I see her sweet little self. This is the love diet.

I now see that little girl as my inner little love bug. My love fairy. She says, *Ooh! I want a cookie. I want to body surf. I want hugs. I want a cute boyfriend. I want to love life. I want a cozy bed. I want it all! I want to be happy. I want to feel cute and innocent and have wonder and adventures and an awesome life.* And I've denied her. I haven't listened to her. I shut her down for a really long friggin' time. I silenced her and bullied her and invalidated her. And nothing (nothing!) pisses me off more than when someone invalidates a woman's needs. Yet here I was, invalidating the shit out of my own basic, sweet, and valid needs. I was my own bully.

☆ ☆ ☆

# TRUST

" **T**RUST YOURSELF!" I WROTE in my last book. What a joke. I haven't trusted myself one single bit lately. I've restricted all aspects of my life for the past three years, trying to heal, trying to get healthy, trying to lose weight, trying to tolerate myself. There was no trust. I doubted my business skills, my appetite, and my ability to be in a relationship. I didn't trust life. I didn't trust God (the worst part), so therefore I couldn't trust myself.

I was driven by fear—fear so big it became crippling. I cut myself off from joy and pleasure and food, all while trying to get a grip, feel OK, and heal this horrible pain in my heart. It didn't work. Turns out starvation and restriction don't heal. News flash! Starvation doesn't heal. What I really wanted was love (better body = more opportunity for love). My heart was hungry. Another revelation: a woman on a diet can't love. She is locked in her mind, her prison, her acting out of her imperfectness. The drive to fix oneself suffocates the heart. I should know.

I thought that if I cut out gluten, dairy, sugar, caffeine, alcohol, joy, living—then maybe I'd be eligible for love. How sad. I was crimping my life line, strangling my oxygen, and imprisoning myself. No wonder my love life went to total hell (more on that later!). I couldn't love. I was choking myself and flipped my heart switch to *off*. Love doesn't flow when your heart is cut off. Basic love law 101!

Now I know that it's about trust. It's about listening to your intuition, your desires. It's believing life is working *for* you. That's a game-changer—believing that life is actually on your side. Life wants love for you. It wants to you be fulfilled, impressed, joyously happy, satisfied, fed, happy with yourself, loved, supported, inspired, encouraged, delighted. Yes, honey. Life wants you to be happy.

This isn't about food, it's about my heart. It always was.

☆ ☆ ☆

# RISK

S PEAKING OF TRUST: THERE is risk. Risk is the opposite of and the answer to struggling with trust. Risk *is* faith. I looked carefully at my trust issues (with myself!) and decided I'm really going to take wild risks. I'm going to leap despite total terror. I'm going to risk it all for love. I'm going to stop dieting and eat whatever I want. I'll risk being fat.

I'm going to start my cookie business (because I *must* believe in my ideas, my intuition, my skills) and risk total financial loss. I'm going to go for love. I'm going to believe in my ability to love and be loved. I'm going to risk heartbreak.

What about what we *do* trust in ourselves? Here's my list:

- I *do* trust my business ideas and sense. I know what people probably want and would like to buy.
- I *do* trust that my heart is pure. I want good things for humanity. Desperately.
- I *do* trust that I can love someone unconditionally.
- I *do* trust that I want to grow, evolve, understand everything better, learn.

It's a short list, as I'm trust-building with myself. But it's a start to at least acknowledge a few things we trust about ourselves. What do you *trust* in yourself??

_____

_____

_____

☆ ☆ ☆

# HAWAII

ONE YEAR AGO, I moved to Hawaii for my daughter's surf life. I had big dreams! She'd start competing, I'd live in paradise, ride a bike, eat pineapple, surf, frolic, get healthier, be free.

It sort of happened at the beginning. But I didn't find instant resolution to all our problems. I went there to have a healing with my daughter's dad. Our relationship wasn't great prior to moving, and I thought this would patch things up. He is married, but I thought we could finally coparent. She could have a dad on the scene, and it would make life easy for me (I had been parenting her on my own for a few years since he moved to Hawaii).

So I was looking for the sweet relief of having another parent in her life. It would ease the burden on me. She's an awesome kid, but we'd had a rocky three years, with a lot of anxiety on her part. I needed her father to participate and help me.

My plans didn't pan out. My relationship with him got worse, and we don't talk. The Hawaii dream petered out, and my health got worse. I couldn't get healthy. I was still feeling thick and bloated and overweight. Everything was exacerbated in Hawaii.

I went on lockdown and tried every diet known to man. I read every diet book I could get my hands on and could not find a solution. Throw in being in Hawaii—the land of tan, hot bodies and sexy surfers and skimpy bathing suits—and my insecurity about an "imperfect body" was off the rails.

I cut it all out again, hard-core. Cleansing! No gluten, dairy, sugar, wine, caffeine—the whole miserable song and dance. I dove into Ayurveda, drank a cleansing tea daily, and did the kitchari cleanse (look it up, I'm too exhausted to explain it). Ayurveda: body, mind, soul! This was the balance I needed. Manage my doshas: that's the ticket!

Every other week or so was a different plan:

- all fruit
- then *no* fruit (too much sugar!)
- all vegetables
- more meat
- no meat
- *no* carbs at all
- vegan
- water fasting
- juice fasting
- all bananas (seriously)
- all raw
- no raw; cooked vegetables only
- all liquid diet
- the elemental diet
- the liver cleanse (I became *obsessed* with the Medical Medium; he became my guru. I read all his books on a loop, nonstop. I was eating apples like crazy and trying to heal my liver to attempt to cure everything. *Zero* fat.)
- intermittent fasting
- vodka instead of wine (less sugar!)
- ginger water all day for my "inner digestive fire"
- celery juice (of course, who isn't trying that?)
- lemon water obsessively
- Hormone Reset diet
- during the coronavirus quarantine, the "whatever diet" (Wine at ten in the morning, yes! Who cares?)
- five weeks of *super* low-calorie vegetable and protein diet with homeopathic "fat loss" drops

Who's not exhausted reading this list? No one. It's impossible to not be exhausted reading this; it is insanity. Insanity doesn't heal shit. It creates chaos and stress. I wanted to feel lovable. I was dieting to feel lovable, and I became stressed out by love.

Turns out, that's not love. Guess what? Stress doesn't cure anything. Love does.

☆ ☆ ☆

# MEANING

What's the point? The point is to be at peace with yourself.
—*Women Who Need Donuts*

OK, WELL, THIS WASN'T happening. I've been at war with myself.

Being at peace with yourself means listening to your inner voice—the cravings, the desires, the needs, the wants. She must be heard. She insists on being heard. Shutting her down is not being at peace. Arguing with her and telling her she's wrong and undeserving is not being at peace. Silencing her is warfare. It is corrosive and blocks all that energy trying to come through.

The inner voice is good energy! It's the energy of love and longing and desire. That's what wants to shine in us—the desire, the hunger, the passion, the fire for life. Being at peace with yourself is saying, "Hell, yes!" to your wants and needs.

God didn't plant these desires in us to tease and torment us. God put them in us to manifest, to express, to experience. God wants us to feel awesome. Dare I say, God wants us to feel … ecstasy. Bold statement. I didn't believe it. But I'm starting to. God wants me to feel downright ecstasy. Being at peace with yourself is allowing good, allowing satisfaction and bliss, allowing an amazing life. Because you're freakin' worth it. There is no other point.

☆ ☆ ☆

# SADNESS

Please fucking cry.
—*Women Who Need Donuts* (paraphrased)

I
T OCCURRED TO ME that sadness has paid my bills. I started a
donut business because I was sad. I was sad that life didn't feel
sweet or awesome. I felt I needed donuts and that if *I* did, the rest
of the world probably needed donuts too. Not just sugar, but the
sweet, comforting, fatty deliciousness of a deep-fried donut.

I needed the nostalgia of an old-world donut shop, and I
desperately needed to feel like life was OK and not so miserable.
So my sadness got me out of bed and forced me to open a donut
shop—to heal my own self, give me hope, and maybe give others
hope.

I say to my daughter, "Use your sadness!" It is not a defect. We
are all terrified of sadness, myself included. But it's a wonderful
messenger. It's a motivator. Use it. As I wrote in *Women Who
Need Donuts*, sadness "is a sign of your big beautiful heart" (that
you care).

My sadness paid the bills, and it will again, but I'm also
betting on love to pay the bills this time around. This is the love
diet.

☆ ☆ ☆

# BEAUTY

WOMEN WANT TO FEEL beautiful, and we aren't encouraged to admit that. We *need* to feel beautiful; it's in our cells. Because the truth of who we are is beauty. You can't feel ugly or less-than or shitty about yourself and conquer the world. You can't love others if you feel imperfect. You can't enjoy your life while believing that you are a wretch. You/we *are* love, we are God, and we are nurturing and softness and power. We want peace, and we create life. We are miraculous creatures, and here's the deal about beauty:

There is *nothing* more beautiful than a woman at peace with herself. It is blinding, fucking beauty. It's like looking directly into the sun.

Being at peace with yourself means you honor your needs and desires—and your *wants*. What do women want? I know what I want:

- insane flavor
- really good wine
- white Christmas lights year-round
- dim lighting and hot dates
- touch
- massage
- sex
- hammocks
- good views
- candles
- adventures
- exploring
- men to plan surprises for me
- gardenias
- spaghetti and meatballs
- sleep

- foot rubs (lots of them!)
- listening to good harmonies
- the sound of the grand piano
- drifting in a boat
- bodysurfing
- fruity drinks
- deep talks
- kissing
- lattes
- good color and feng shui
- a good memoir
- nice hotels
- documentaries that inspire
- dancing
- romance
- charming, quirky places
- nature
- a nice car

This is just a start.

Healing begins when you live the life you actually want.
—Claudia Welch

★  ★  ★

# MUSIC

Music that soothes my soul:

- Feist, "Cicadas and Gulls"

    This song is a rare thing in that it brings up both sadness and hope. The sadness is more of a longing that feels so good because not many things can blur the lines of sadness and hope. I love this song.

- Mary J. Blige and U2, "One"

    The best of all time.

- Ray Charles, "Georgia on My Mind"

    The other best song ever written? I think so.

- Anything by Chopin

- Jennifer Hudson, "Moan"

    So sexy, it's almost uncomfortable. It's like, "'Moan?' Are we allowed to do that? Pure primal satisfaction? Oh God, I didn't think I was allowed." Listen to this song immediately.

- Loren Alfred, "Never Enough"

    It's never enough (flavor, pleasure, touch). Sorry. I want it all.

- Emma Jean Foster, "Keep Your Loving Arms around Me"

Gospel. God is #1. God is our first and primary parent. God's arms are there for us. I am in love with this visual. I meditate on God hugging me, embracing me in the storm, reminding me that I am supported, held. He won't let me down. He just won't.

- Anything by Cynthia Erivo. She is a vocal goddess. I am obsessed.

- Bahamas, "Lost in the Light"

  Soothing, easy song. I need to be lost in the light as often as possible.

- JP Cooper, "Love in the Silence"

  My song about faith in love. That even when people are distant and not talking, there is love.

- Dram, H.E.R., Watt, "The Lay Down"

  Oh God, such a ridiculously sexy song. It oozes passion. This is my theme song when trying to manifest romance.

- Thirdstory with Eryn Allen Kane, "Still in Love" (acoustic)

  This song is so sexy too. It hits in on *every* cylinder for me. The voices, the soul, the piano. Holy shit.

- H.E.R. … anything by this genius.

- Birdtalk, "Lover"

This song confirms my belief in beautiful love. I still try to understand the concept of having a lover—another person committed to connecting physically and spiritually to just one person to bring each other love and pleasure in the body. It is sacred. Two bodies committed to each other's comfort and pleasure. It is so scary and vulnerable. I want all that: the pleasure, the scary, and the vulnerable. I'll take it all.

- Adam Levine and Alicia Keys, "Wild Horses"

  The power of this song! It's the power of love. The physical force of love is captured in this song like no other. This is the love I want and what I feel with John. I fought for it. Now that we have it, nothing will stop it. The love force is on.

- Juxtaposition, "River"

  This. Song. Is. Me. If we could define ourselves in one song, this is it! This is the real me. Gospel, faith, soul. I well up with tears when I hear this song. *This song is the real me.*

Find things that sum you up. What is *your* "real me"?

☆ ☆ ☆

# WINE

W INE SOOTHES MY SOUL. In *Women Who Need Donuts*, I talked about my conflicted relationship with wine. My need to reduce, my need to temper the desire for wine, because I want it too much. I felt forced to institute a 1.5-to 2-glass maximum. "Pray more, drink less," I wrote. I still pray a lot. But I need wine. It's just a fact.

The wine restriction was the worst part of my past three years of personal dietary lockdown. Suppressing my appetite for it, I felt like a starving caged animal with a hunk of meat outside of the metal bars taunting me every time I'd look at it. It was my personal hell.

I've felt torn because wine is my love. I just didn't know how to incorporate it into my health plan. That is, until recently.

I started learning about the Tao, "The Way." It talks about the *middle*—letting the pendulum stay in the middle, not swinging one way to the far left or far right. This has not been my approach to wine. During this crazy diet phase I'd been on, I'd abstain, abstain, abstain, then when I would have alcohol, I'd drink way too much. Just recently, after four or five weeks of a diet/cleanse deal, I'd been refraining from alcohol. Then I went out with friends and had multiple glasses of wine. I told my mom about it, and she said, "Oh, so you binged."

It hit me: that old behavior was still in my bag of tricks. Restrict myself from something I love, and sure as hell, the pendulum will swing the other way, big time. The key is to stay in the middle. Have a glass of wine. Every day is OK. It's better than being crazy and extreme and holding off from something for weeks on end, then going wild when the chains come off. It's chaos and totally absurd.

The Tao has restored my sanity. Stay in the middle. Have what I want every day, a little bit or even more. The pendulum swinging wildly makes me crazy. We can't do crazy anymore. The world doesn't need any more crazy.

# ☆ ☆ ☆
# PLEASURE LOG

T HIS IS THE MOST exciting and life-changing part of this story. It hit me just a few days ago that I need to document my pleasure. The past three years, I've been writing *daily* about my diet, my restriction, my food revelations. Yes, there was a lot of positive stuff along the way, including personal insights. But the dialogue was mostly restriction, keeping track of my progress through cutting out *everything*.

I hit my wall. It came over me like a tidal wave. "This is not working! All this restriction is suffocating me! It's sucking the ever-loving life out of me. I have myself in a straightjacket, and I'm about to explode." In one day, I went from lockdown, imprisoned Leigh to *free* Leigh. God's voice inside me told me to let myself out of jail.

I exonerated myself. I liberated the love fairy in me and declared that I'm going to trust this little voice, the desire, the appetite, and the fairy. I'm going to free her, and I'm going to *trust* her. I don't need to live in self-imposed jail another minute, starting with lunch.

And there I was: a free woman. I decided to try one week of saying *yes* to life, and I started logging.

## Day One

*I happened to be on an island this day.*

Wake up, coffee! Soy milk … yum. I haven't let myself have these things in a long time. Soy milk is the most symbolic example of food confusion. It's good for you! It's terrible for you. It causes cancer … it doesn't cause cancer! It screws up your hormones; it balances your hormones. I've had it. I'm drinking soy milk because I love it. I no longer listen to the experts. I follow my own advice. What you love will love you back, right? I'd like to think so.

Then I had eggs with lobster and butter and toast (nope, weren't allowed any of this stuff on any previous diet plans either).

I went on a long, slow hike—*not* to burn calories but to soak in the scenery, to be alone, to listen to the silence and then the wind, feel the sun, and play my favorite music. I sat for a while midhike on the cliff. I meditated with my thoughts. Took my time. Thought about John. As I meandered home, I found a rock that had *Be Love* painted on it. Of course. I had been saying this to myself for days.

I took a long nap. I let myself rest. That's not easy for some of us, and definitely not me. I was lost in dreams for a few hours.

I had a latte. My favorite, most comforting thing.

We boarded the boat to come home. I wrapped myself in a cozy scarf and read a book for the long boat ride. I was enjoying my *self*, settling into myself.

Got home and cracked the *good* bottle of wine, the one I'd been saving. I had two luscious glasses and enjoyed every sip along with the most delicious dinner of blackened shrimp, rice with butter, and garlicky kale.

I had a day dripping with pleasure and personal satisfaction—not always my norm. I really *can* let go, give into my compass, and say, "Just enjoy, honey. Have the good wine. Drink the latte. Nap a long nap in the middle of a sunny day. It's all good."

It felt like a true miracle. I felt like I had come home to myself. For the love of God, may we all please come home to ourselves.

## Day Two

Tea. Fruit salad with yogurt and granola. My soul food. I love this.

I had my favorite toast and eggs again. Lots of butter. And once again, a new indulgence.

I went to meet someone at my favorite coffee shop with the *best* almond-milk lattes. I had one of their famous scones. No more avoiding gluten. I dipped the scone in the latte and said fuck it to carb loading. This was a big deal for me. I enjoyed every crumb and every sip. Bravo!

I went to see my best friend Susanne. We sat in her backyard and spilled our hearts as usual. We are soul sisters. She is my lifeline. Our visit today was soul food.

I took my mom out to dinner. We haven't done that since the quarantine. It was magic. We went to a waterfront deck. She had Manhattans, I had two glasses of delicious French wine. I ordered four entrées! I said, "Mom, we are celebrating that I don't diet anymore. Let's order what we want, then take home whatever we don't eat and have delicious leftovers tomorrow." It was a feast.

I gave her an update on John. I told her I had figured it out. John was having a terrible time trusting me after the Hawaii debacle, of course. He said, "I love you, but I don't trust you." Which enraged me. I was pissed at him for saying that, so I said, "You *still* don't trust me? I love you! What do I have to do? What do I have to say?"

Then I realized, there is nothing to say. I don't trust *myself* for shit. I don't trust myself! I say I do, but it's a farce. I don't trust my loving-ness or my business skills or my capabilities or my freakin' appetite *or* my total ability to commit to him. I slept on it and had a realization. He shouldn't trust me, because I have never trusted myself. It's basic law: we can't deeply trust someone whose own foundation isn't solid.

I transformed with this realization. I found my balls (sorry, this is a guy anatomy reference, but it works). I said to myself, *Find your truth, girl—your inner trust, your cojones, your power, or you're going to keep bottoming out in relationships.* It clicked. I said, "I'm going to trust it all, mostly my appetite!" *No. More. Dieting.* (What I really want is love.)

And my mom and I went out to dinner to celebrate. I got it. No one better to celebrate my liberation with than my mother.

## Day Three

I woke up and made a mocha. My favorite! This had been a forbidden treat.

Coffee, chocolate, agave, and soy milk. Luscious.

I went to an acupuncture appointment. I had a new therapist. Oh my God, I found my healer. His name is Johnathan, and he is such a gentle soul I just melted with him. I was so open and talked about my past three years of health struggles. He absorbed it with compassion, a gentle touch, and a confident intuition that I just ate up. I drifted into relaxation and felt like I was led to this person for major healing.

He did cupping on me too, and I felt completely comforted in his care. He will help me clear my blockages and stuck places and restore my energy flow of love and life energy. Life is so good; it steers us to the right people.

I came home and warmed up those leftovers from my dinner with my mom and savored every amazing bite. I had a glass of that good wine from a few days earlier. And it hit me as I was warming up all the food. My brain kept saying, *Oh, I get this?* I realized I am reprogramming myself for joy, allowance, pleasure, and abundance. It is *so* symbolic for life. I was warming up these seared scallops, and I thought, *Oh, I get this?*

What had happened to me along the way? What the hell happened the last three years that turned my pleasure channel off?

I don't know! But I am now saying *yes* to life. I am allowing myself to say *yes* to life! In all ways: in love, in scallops, in experiences, in comfort, in pleasure, in wine, in abundance. No more restriction. No more holding back. It's just over. I've had a miraculous renewal.

## Day Four

Ah, a mocha. So crazy good. I love this. Sad to have denied this coffee passion for so long. Chocolate and coffee combined are my love.

John and I decided to buy a boat! He found one in Boston, so we took a road trip. We loaded up on lattes and a cooler of delicious food and headed south. He had been dreaming of a boat throughout our years together, and something just clicked this week. We have been rekindling our relationship, and it felt right to just pull the trigger and commit to something big together.

We took a quick cruise in the boat, and I said yes to the guy, counted the cash out, gleefully jumped in the car with a new boat trailered on, and headed back to Maine in total euphoria. We talked ad nauseum about all the ways we were going to enjoy our new boating life together. Explorations! Water-skiing! Coolers of amazing food and cocktails at sunset with our best friends on this boat.

John was aglow. We both felt exuberant joy and hope for life. Passion was restored, and life felt magical. This boat is the best thing that's ever happened. Then we had dinner.

We went to our favorite place for wine, crispy brussels sprouts, and seared scallops. We continued to talk in stream of consciousness. John and I never stop talking.

It was an amazing day.

I am in love.

## Day Five

I woke up so early.

I was at John's, and I came home before sunrise. I had *two* mochas. I'm really letting go! I love this self-love thing. It is so much better than dieting.

Today was our maiden voyage on the new boat. The weather was stellar: bright sun and hot as hell. The water glistened, and John, his kids, and two of my best friends and I all had such palpable excitement about this adventure. We all needed joy, adventure, sun on our face, and Lord, mostly we've all needed hope. This boat was bought to restore hope. To restore hope in fun. To restore hope in letting go and in life!

Cruising around the sparkling bay, weaving in and out of the islands, sipping a beer, blasting reggae, and soaking in life, there is no choice but to let go. No more stress from now on. This past many months have been stressful for all humanity. If we can loosen up and melt right into a pleasurable life, everybody wins. I'm naming the boat the SS *Pleasure.*

We stopped at a friend's house on an island for a glass of wine. He gave us a bunch of lobsters he'd just caught and cooked. Could life get any better?

We got home and cracked the lobster. John's older son, Elijah, and I cooked. He cracked the lobster, and I chopped garlic and made pasta with alfredo sauce. He and I gently eased into conversation, as I haven't been in their life since the big breakup. He mentioned a friend who just died, a kid his own age, nineteen. It was a car accident, but Elijah was speculating it was intentional. I was surprised at the conversation topic but intrigued to hear his thoughts.

"The thought of a teenager committing suicide shatters my heart," I said.

He said, "You know, I'm realizing this is all temporary. The *being in the body* thing." He was alluding to the value he sees in the time spent on Earth.

"Yes!" I said. "Exactly! Being human is freakin' hard, but it's also a gift! A crazy, magical, sacred gift. The body is the pleasure vessel. It is meant to be enjoyed. The earth is a miracle; it is also meant to be enjoyed. Taste, smell, touch, feel the breeze on your body, marvel at nature. Watch a flock of birds move into formation silently in the sky and try not to be amazed by the intelligence and beauty of the universe. This experience on planet Earth is a gift."

And I reminded Elijah, "When your dad's brother died, he came to their sister in a dream and said, 'I want my skin back.' That says it all. Our time in the skin is gold. It is holy. It is our time to live as an expression of God—the ecstatic, joyful miraculous expression of God." I added, "To anyone who doesn't soak up the experience of life on Earth, joke's on them."

I know some people have a really hard time. I get that, and I have compassion. But for those of us who are blessed, all we have to do is say thank you to God and enjoy our blessings.

We had the lobster alfredo with some killer Italian red wine. I sopped it up with black-olive bread dipped in oil, salt, and pepper—my favorite.

Life … you're *so* good to me.


## Day Six

Couldn't wait to get out of bed for a mocha … delicious every time.

I went for a long walk on the beach this morning. This is my favorite time. Walking, breathing, thinking, looking at the waves before doing anything else for the day. It is really not about burning calories anymore. It is just about being alive.

I met Susana for coffee. We compared notes on the ways we continuously are both elevating our self-love. It's such a marathon. Such a process. Every day, we commit to acting with more love. More love. More love. More love.

We went out on the boat. Another awesome day. We drifted in the rocks. Oops. John wasn't paying attention; I alerted him, and he went into panic mode. I didn't move. I was consciously aware that I didn't need to do anything, I knew he'd handle it, and he did. He's totally competent. It was my moment to realize I trust him completely. It was a turning point. He's my man.

I came home to make the most delicious dinner: salmon, kale, and quinoa. I can't even comprehend food guilt anymore. It's miraculous. It's just become clear I need to eat. As soon as I said to my therapist last week, "I have an eating disorder," it's like God swooped in and fixed my brain. "Eat," he said. "Just effing eat."

Reflecting on last week when I said the words out loud, "I have an eating disorder," it was one of the scariest confessions I've ever made. And with that declaration, the healing began, and fast. *The truth heals.*

I need to fuel this beautiful being. I will no longer mind-fuck myself—craving something and then guilt-tripping myself about it. I am done with that. I demand satisfaction in *all* areas. I will no longer tolerate not being satisfied. You can't do shit in this world with an empty tank. You can't do shit in this world if you're hungry. You can't do shit in this world if you're starving your soul of what you need and what you crave. It's almost comical that for so long I thought I could torture myself and thrive. Poor me—I know better now.

## Day Seven

A week of saying *yes* to life—I did it!

Wake up ... mocha!

I spent half the day with my business partner looking for locations to sell our cookies (my new business). It was productive! We are going to get this business going soon.

It was so intensely hot today, I decided to give up on being productive for the second half of the day. Susana and I met at my mom's pool. It turned into a magical day of floating, listening to a blend of R&B and opera, and talking for hours with my mom. We talked about our usual topics: life, spirituality, our childhood traumas, self-love, our relationship questions, our children's issues, and world concerns. No, we don't do small talk.

We made martinis and felt, *Is this real life?* All of us felt constant gratitude. We are blessed, and we know it.

We made martinis. They had dirty martinis with olives, but I like fruity things. I made a grapefruit version, and it was bliss.

We needed food, but my mom's fridge was (unusually) bare. We scrounged together what she had and made tuna melts—a rare treat. We enjoyed the evening breeze with our cocktails and tuna melts, and I felt quite good that this week was a success. Two of my favorite women, warm air, cocktails, and snacks. One of the last things my dad said before he died was, "When things are good, let them be good."

Life is good. I had been overcomplicating things for so long, battling with myself. I've dropped the swords. I've relaxed. I've eased back into life.

Martinis, tuna melts, people I love.

Simple, easy.

Life.

# SHOULDS

T HE PLEASURE LOG IS the opposite of the approach I've always had. I've always had a voice of *shoulds* in my head, like a screaming drill sergeant. I'd allowed the drill sergeant to run the show. "You *should* go for a run today. You *should* avoid carbs. You *should not* reach out to the man in your life—you don't want to be too much. You *should* make dinner for your new neighbors to show them that you are a good person. You *should* clean the house so people don't think you're a slob."

What if I don't feel like doing any of these things? What if I just want to be? I decided to change the rules of the *should* game:

- Waiter: "Ma'am, would you like another glass of wine?"

  Me: "Yes! I think I should!"

- Waiter: "Madam, how about some dessert?"

  Me: "Wonderful idea, I probably *should* have the chocolate torte, yes!"

- Husband: "Honey, do you think you need a bath or a massage?"

  Me: "Absolutely yes! I most certainly *should*!"

And instead of saying, "I *should* go for a run," I say, "Boy, I'd really enjoy a run." Because that actually is often true. I love getting energy out, listening to hip-hop, and jogging through the streets watching the world go by. I used to do it because my inner drill sergeant told me to burn calories, but not recently. I'm changing that old story. I actually *like* to move, because I'm alive.

And am I the only one who says, upon eating with others sometimes, "Oh I haven't eaten all day"? As if to have to justify the need to eat? Enough of that. Just shut the f up and eat. Trust your appetite for everything: life, relationships, affection, inspiration, happiness.

> We need to eat with gusto and passion like
> women who are not afraid of their appetite.
> —*Women Who Need Donuts*

These positive *shoulds* don't roll off of most of our tongues naturally at all. In fact, saying "Yes, I should" feels like speaking another language when responding to an offer of wine or chocolate cake. I'm ready to reprogram my brain. I can't live in the old version of *should*. I was strangled. I now play the *should* game daily! It's fun.

☆ ☆ ☆

# LOVE

T HIS IS THE MOST complicated part of the book. Ironic. "Love should be easy!" my mother said recently. Really? Because love has been the most challenging part of my existence so far. Fascinating, but fully true.

Twelve years ago, I was married. I had a four-year-old and worked in a restaurant in Portland, Maine. My husband (whom I'd met when living in California) and I had moved here to Maine after he'd lost a job. We came here to build a house in the woods with solar power, his dream. And I wanted to be closer to my family. I worked in a restaurant while he basically lived in the woods and hand-built a house.

One night after work, I went to another restaurant for a drink. I ordered a glass of white wine and was served by a man in a crisp white shirt with the most beautiful face I'd ever seen. I was stunned. *Who is this bartender?* I thought.

His name was John. He was easy, chatty, charming, and handsome. I was married, but I was captivated. I drank my wine and went home. The guy crossed my mind, but I was married. I asked my friend about him—she worked with him at the bar— and she said, "He's great. He's also married. Two kids."

"OK, well, he's cute," I said. He certainly got my attention.

Four years passed.

I had just opened my first donut shop. I was slaving away the first few weeks, making the donuts alone and trying to keep up with the budding business. It was just me, my dad, and one or two employees. My sister was involved in the shop too, but this day she was home monitoring our Facebook page.

I was flipping donuts that morning when my phone dinged. A text came from my sister that said, "You just got a message on our business Facebook page. It's from some John guy." She misspelled his last name, but I immediately wondered if it was the John from four years ago at the bar. I dropped my donut sticks midfry and ran to the back office to check the computer. It was him!

He said, "I don't know what's going on in your life, but I wonder if you'd like to meet for a drink or a walk or whatever."

I wrote back, "Yes! Yes, I do!"

I had just gotten divorced, and apparently he had too. The stars had aligned. We were both available, and he was asking me out on an actual date. I was elated.

A day or two later, he called me. No text—an actual phone call. Sadly, this is rare, but I loved that he called for the first-date planning. The donut shop had just closed when he called, and the place was empty. We had a big leather couch for customers to lounge on, and I answered the call and flopped on the couch. I remember every bit of the conversation.

I remember really observing the tone of his voice and his choice of words. I remember his humor and his forthrightness about our plans. "We'll go for a walk at Mackworth Island, how about that?" The day that we first talked was Easter Sunday. "Let's go out Wednesday," he said. "I'll pick you up."

"Great," I said. "I'll see you Wednesday."

☆ ☆ ☆

On Wednesday, when he picked me up, I was nervous but so excited. We took a short drive across a bridge to an island and set out on a walk. The island is beautiful. It's right off the coast of our little town, so you feel like you're on an adventure but really just a few minutes from civilization. We strolled and had easy conversation.

After we had walked for a few minutes, he said, "Let's just sit."

We hiked down a short path and sat on the rocks overlooking the water. It was warm, sunny, and quite magical. We lingered on the rocks for only a few minutes, and then he said, "You wanna leave and go get a drink?"

"Yes!" I said. (A guy who likes nature but really just wants a martini? I loved it!) "Let's go!"

So off we went. Nature time was over. He suggested this swanky little Thai place in town. This date was awesome so far. I was loving it.

We got the perfect table in the window. I got a blueberry vodka lemonade thing, and he got bourbon and then a beer. We talked easily about our kids, our divorces, life. He ordered some apps. I sat there engaged in the flowing conversation; I was really just studying his face and thinking to myself as he talked, *This is it. This is my guy. I'm never going on another date again. I'm done. I found him.*

We wrapped up the snacks and, after another couple of drinks, he said, "Do you want to go make out?"

"Yes!" I said. "Please!"

So we swiftly departed and walked toward his car. Along the way, we stopped behind another restaurant, and he kissed me. It was electric. We made out, and it totally overtook every part of my being. I was ignited. It was the best first kiss ever.

*Oh my God, I'm so done*, I thought. *I'm done.* I loved every second of it. We went to his house and kissed more. I stayed over. The next day, he drove me home, and I was in like. Major like. I floated into the donut shop to get to work. I was a woman in love.

He texted me later. There were no games. We talked a lot the next few days. I don't remember our next few dates at all, but within a couple of days, I was at the beach just sitting and he called and said, "Where are you?" I told him my location and within minutes, I saw him running toward me. He blasted into my beach lounging area with his two kids sitting in his car in the parking lot and burst out, "Will you be my girlfriend?"

"Yes! I will!" I said without hesitation. And he ran off.

I felt euphoric. I loved this question, and I loved his forthrightness. I wanted to be his girlfriend. I resumed my sitting and staring at the ocean, and I glowed. Things felt great. And so began our journey.

The next few months brought on the phase of our single-parent dating life. Every Thursday night for months, we had a date night. We never missed it. All our kids were with their other parent on Thursday, so that was John's and my night to hang out at his apartment and cook dinner together and talk. I'd usually haul over a bag of groceries and margarita supplies, and we'd cook and eat and watch a movie. I was always exhausted because I did the early morning donut production daily, but I'd cook, slug down a few margaritas, then pass out on his couch or crawl to his bed alone. These were our dates. Not too exciting, but I loved it.

Within about four months, we had decided to rent a house together and move into it with our three kids. We found a cool place and made the move.

I thought playing house would be great, and I remember before the move looking at his face and thinking, *Yes, this is the face I want to look at forever. It feels like home.* So off we went into a house across town to blend our lives and start something together.

It was a disaster.

Within a few weeks, I realized I wasn't ready for this. I was working a million hours a week at the donut shop. I was a ball of anxiety about the business and all the demands it presented. I wanted to come home and go catatonic most days, be alone, stew in my anxiety and my exhaustion and just be.

Instead, I'd come home to a house full of people. Three kids instead of one. A new partner I didn't know that well yet, and a new set of responsibilities I felt totally overwhelmed by. I was suddenly the mom of the house, and I was barely hanging on. I could barely manage myself and my new business. I was spread way too thin.

I'd retreat into my room often, reading magazines and avoiding everyone. Obviously, this was not well received. I just needed some breathing room, and I didn't know how to ask for it. The resentment and the separation between me and John was building fast.

One night, we walked across the street to our favorite little restaurant for dinner and sat at the bar. We chatted about my business, and he said he wanted to do a project there for me. I said, "Sure! Let's make a plan." Something about my response set off his inner fire alarm, and an explosion happened between us. The mounting tension erupted. My response felt disrespectful to him. I didn't totally get it, but we were both so triggered we could barely speak to ask for the bill. We got it, paid, and quickly left. We walked home and launched into the worst fight of our relationship. It was horrific. He told me I was terrible and didn't respect him.

The next day I said, "I'm moving out."

I packed up, found an apartment for my daughter and me, and fled.

Fast forward a few months. John and I had talked intermittently after I'd moved, but it was tense and emotional. He couldn't understand why I left.

I explained that I can't do conflict, and that was that.

One night, while I was making meatballs in my new apartment, he called and said, "I miss you."

I said, "Me too! I really miss you."

And so began the next seven years of our love struggle.

We got back together and broke up many more times. It was always the same. Get back together ... stay in the happy zone for months ... then have these catastrophic flare-ups that were always a result of me saying something to him that I thought was constructive criticism and he took as just criticism. We would both flare. It was a cycle of insanity that (I now see) was just a sign of our inner triggers being poked at, our inner unworthiness.

He would always ask me for more love, saying he didn't feel I was loving him enough. And I'd get pissed and say, "Fuck you! I love you enough." And I'd throw him out.

It's sad. It's comical. Fighting about love. But that was the best we could do. And we continued this crazy cycle for seven years.

☆ ☆ ☆

Then I moved to Hawaii for my daughter to have better waves. We decided John would come too. He would close his business in Maine and move to Hawaii. We would get engaged, and we would seal the deal. We would start a new life.

I got a head start and went in August. He had loose ends to wrap up, and he'd come in October. I was fifty-fifty about the whole plan. I knew I loved him. I also knew the seven-year cycle of love games we'd been playing still didn't sit right with me. I questioned our stability, and I questioned whether getting married was a wise thing to do.

He'd call and I'd say, "I love you! I can't wait for you to get to Hawaii!" But I was being a fake. I *did* want that, but I also really questioned the whole thing.

Then he showed up. He came with a wedding ring and all his belongings and was bursting with energy for this new, easy, tropical life. And he came with his two kids.

Within days, I felt suffocated. I felt totally unable to commit, and I threw him out. Yes, I bounced him off the island. I said, "Go back to Maine. I'm not doing this."

I botched it. I did the worst thing anyone could do to someone. I told him one thing while feeling another. I lied. I broke his heart. I mind-fucked his kids. And I did it because I wanted to. I also did it out of pain. I couldn't get married because I wasn't ready, and John took the hit.

It was a catastrophe.

Months went by, and we talked a little. I felt self-righteous about my decision and could not see how much damage I'd done. I remained in my Hawaii life doing my thing. Long walks, smoothies, taking care of my daughter. I was in la-la land.

Then John and I started talking again, really talking. I started reading books about relationships and diving into the mess that had become of ours. I was illuminated. I confessed one day that I had no idea how to just *be*. "I'm so terrified of just *being* with you," I told him, "of being boring."

"You can be boring," he said. "I want you to be boring." I was relieved.

All the years of our love battles were just signs of our inner children (cliché, I know) crying out for help. He felt unlovable. I know I sure did. I felt totally unlovable. I always thought that he would eventually abandon me. He felt the same. Our cries for help always resulted in an explosion because we were both needy and just wanted love, and never knew how to ask for it.

So here we were at the grand finale, in Hawaii, when I threw him out, acting out (my) shit. It was him and an engagement ring and me responding, "You don't love me! Leave!" Because I didn't believe he loved me or that anyone could love me.

All the books I read got me changing. I looked at myself

under a magnifying glass. I started to totally understand myself and him, really clearly. I saw his little-boy self, wanting love and freaking out whenever he didn't feel loved by me. And I saw the same thing in me. In retrospect, I wish we could have always just said, "Hey, could you provide a little more love? Thanks!" But we never knew how to do that. We'd both just explode, or retreat, or give up. We didn't know any better.

So I came back from Hawaii after almost a year. And he said, "Um, I'm dating someone else."

I felt like I was going to puke. I took a deep breath but really, I lost my shit.

I said, "OK, that's fair. I dumped you. You should be dating someone else."

And part of me really meant that. The other part of me started to totally panic. I went into total recon mode and dug way the fuck into these feelings that surfaced in me at the thought of losing John. I literally went into *panic* mode.

I felt untethered. I felt lost. I felt adrift. I felt fatherless. I felt godless. I felt abandoned and terrified. I felt *terrified*.

I thought, *I can't do this! I can't do any of this! I can't do life. I have no one. I have no father. I have no man in my life at all. I have no one to call when I need help. No one.* John had been my lifeline for a long time, the person I could call at all hours and he was always available. Always. And he was now dating someone else. Despite the fact that I'd dumped him and broken off the engagement, I was feeling the consequences of my choices. I was petrified.

He gave me no relief, really, from my grief. He had moved on, and I sat at home for those few weeks and sobbed. I sat in my tub for weeks and sobbed my guts out. I sobbed because I felt so alone. I sobbed because I had no belief in myself to do life alone. I sobbed because I'd fucked up the closest thing I'd ever had to love. I sobbed because I'd lost my best friend. I sobbed that my dad was dead. I sobbed as I questioned if life would really end up OK. I sobbed that I'd be single forever and just die a miserable, lonely death, and there was no such thing as a happy ending.

I had to let all this shit out. All this stuff had been dormant in me my whole life, and I had never felt it. It came rushing to the surface, all as a result of the possibility of losing John. I had lost him, and the volcano erupted. The volcano in me burst forth with a lava of pain, sadness, terror, loneliness, unworthiness, and lack of faith. It was a shit show, and it was *excruciating*.

Then one day I talked to John. We both said we still loved each other.

I was driving, and I had to pull over.

I said, "I love you!"

He said, "I love you too!"

I thought we had figured it out. But we hadn't. He was still dating someone else, and it tormented me.

Weeks went by again. There was more sludge in my heart. I just wanted him to love me. I thought I was ready to love him. I wasn't.

There were more tears. I said to myself, "For the love of God, will the tears ever end?"

What the hell did I have to do here to get over my fears about being alone and living life without a man? Apparently, I had to believe in myself. That was still unresolved, and I was in denial that I could do it. I wanted John to anesthetize me, to prove I was lovable, to stop the bleeding in my being. I was hemorrhaging with insecurity.

I cried more for days. I sobbed. I prayed. I assessed my thoughts about my own abilities and made peace with myself and my life. Then the tears dried up.

John and I went for a walk on the beach. He was single again. He said, "We are not doing this the old way."

I said, "Hell no. We don't need to. Let's get to know each other again. Who are you now?"

He said, "I'm rebuilding. Hawaii really fucked me."

I said, "I know. I'm sorry. Can you forgive me?"

He said, "I don't know."

"Fair," I said.

And we walked.

Then we kissed, just a brief peck on the lips.

"Tangerine," I said.

That was a code word we'd made up years prior sitting at a restaurant in a rare and honest moment when we confessed that we both often question if the other person really loves us. One of us randomly said, "*Tangerine.* That's our secret code word for 'In case you forget, or you doubt it, *tangerine* means *I do love you.*"

So we had a beach walk. "Tangerine," I texted after.

Slowly rebuilding again.

I couldn't wait for another kiss.

Then a few more days went by. He stopped by unannounced. We connected finally. He kissed me, and I felt like I could breathe again. I was dying and suffocating without touching him for so many months. Dramatic, I know, but I'm a hot-blooded woman, and I've always been so attracted to him. I need physical attraction; it fuels my fire, and he does it for me.

We made out. I melted. I felt relief. I can't live without love. He feels like my other half. This has been hard-earned love. *Not* easy love. It's been a battle, a shit show. We had to burn it to the ground in Hawaii, and regrettably there were a bunch of kids caught in the cross fire, but the total inferno led to a new love that is fresh and pure and resurrected.

I hope ultimately the kids can see that sometimes love cracks people wide open, and not always in a good way. But that it can be restored, that there can be happy endings, and that good people can refuse to give up on each other. My previous belief that love stories don't exist was wrong. I proved myself wrong. Love wins and is real. My heart is on fire. We might have an actual love story.

☆ ☆ ☆

# DAD

M Y DAD WAS MY donut angel. In 2011, I started my donut business, and it grew so fast he jumped in to help within a few months. He said, "You have a business on your hands, and you can't afford to pay anyone." He started showing up every single day at six a.m. I'd fry donuts, and he'd run around my seven a.m. deliveries. We laughed that he was my "donut donkey." He did it with a smile on his face, and together we launched a business. We opened three shops.

He was a saint and a huge help for years. He did everything: fix the equipment, run the cash register, sweep the floor, get supplies. Whatever I needed, I'd call, and he'd jump to it. We both loved the excitement of a new business.

About five years in, he started to look different. He lost weight, lost his taste for beer (weird red flag!), and got sluggish. He'd been diagnosed with pancreatic cancer but had decided to keep it all a secret. He endured the trauma of chemo. He stayed home a few days a week and suffered through the chemo effects, then he'd bounce back and report to the donut shop to help. He was a champ. He couldn't help himself: he loved the Holy Donut. He was proud and just all in to see that it worked.

His health started to decline. He could barely eat. We'd been in denial about his inevitable death because he was so good at faking being OK.

Then he died.

I write a lot about the death process in *Women Who Need Donuts*, but in retrospect, there were some notable things about his death that I've recently been thinking about. The night he died in hospice, we had all just left his room. I went home to go to sleep. He seemed fine; unconscious, but we'd thought he'd live through the night, so we all went home. I was in bed, and my daughter was at my mother's house.

My sister called and said, "You need to come get Avery. She

said she's overwhelmed with the feeling that you have to go back to hospice *right now.*"

I said, "What? We just left, I'll go back in the morning."

"No," my sister said. "Avery said come now, pick her up. Go see Dad *now.*"

"Uh, OK," I said. I got dressed, got out of bed, and drove across town for Avery, and back we went to hospice.

My cousin was sitting with my dad. She had just lost both her parents, so she was very familiar with the dying process. She said, "Your dad is fine; his breathing is strong. I'll leave you alone with him. I love you. Have a good night."

And so she left. Avery and I sat on either side of my unconscious father. I just looked at him, and I put my hand on his wrist. I was feeling his pulse. Within minutes, his breathing changed. He gasped, and he took his last breath. I felt his pulse stop. I'd never seen anyone die. My father had just died six inches from my face. I calmly, in response to his stopped pulse, said, "Ave, please go out to the car and get my phone. Please don't question me; just go now and get it."

I called my mom first. I said, "Mom, Dad stopped breathing."

The whole family tore across town and burst into the room.

My sister and I both collapsed on my father and let out the most primal, unfamiliar sobs I'd ever heard. I didn't know what these unrecognizable sounds were that were coming out of us. We heaved on him like animals. I had lost my father.

The tears flooded out. Then we stood in a circle: my mom, my sister and her husband, our kids. My dad's spirit rose up. We stood in silence, then we slowly filtered out of the room. I was the last to go. I couldn't leave. I knew it was the last time with my father's body.

"Bye, Dad," I said. And I went home.

Three years later, I started talking to my mom about our life.

"So … let's talk about John," I said. "I refused his marriage proposal. I don't get love. I feel like a mess. Thoughts?"

She and my father had married each other three times, divorced twice. Maybe there was a clue here.

I remember the first divorce. I was two years old. My dad moved out, and I have some memory of the moment. I was sitting with my sister in the bathroom, and she said, "Dad's leaving. He's moving out."

"Oh, OK," I said. I remember being aware of what was going on but not emotional about it at all.

What I didn't realize is that he'd move in and out many more times over the next many years. I don't remember; maybe it was just normal for me from ages two through, I think, seven.

My mom said, "Yes, Dad moved in and out all the time. He'd love me one day, then not the next."

"Wow," I said. "I really don't remember that."

"Yeah," she said. "That was your childhood." She continued, "He couldn't make up his mind."

*My God*, I thought. *How confusing for my mother.* And heartbreaking! I felt compassion for her. And I could see why I didn't believe in love.

Then, when I was eleven years old, my dad decided he did love her, and they started dating again. It was like a miracle. I never saw it coming; I was fully used to the broken family life. We'd go back and forth between their two apartments, then all of a sudden, my dad said, "We're getting married again. I'm buying a great house, and life is back together!"

I was overjoyed. My faith in life and love and fairy tales was restored. My family was back together, and I felt like I could breathe again.

They seemed happy for nine years. Then one day, they said,

"We're getting divorced again. We're selling this house. *And* everything is fine!"

*It's not fine*, I thought. I collapsed on the floor and sobbed from the depths of my soul.

"See?" I said to life. "There really is no such thing as love. Everything always bottoms out. Families aren't real. There is nothing to believe in and life sucks."

That was my deepest belief. I'd lost hope. My mental computer was now programmed. Love was not real. And my heart was now broken.

Then off I went trying to make believe I could fake it through a relationship.

I dumped John in Hawaii because I had no faith in love. I had zero confidence in marriage or love sticking around or husbands and wives who make it work. I thought men would come and go and people just get sick of each other and that's that.

I have since restored myself. I do have faith in love. I do believe people can be unconditional with each other and love each other despite their doubts and wounds. The happy ending my parents *did* have was my mother nursed my dad through his entire dying process. They healed their relationship. My father died in love.

I need to believe that things work out. I do have faith in love and families and never giving up on someone. Love *is* easy, actually. Trust love.

# BEING SIXTEEN

A VERY WAS THIRTEEN WHEN I wrote *Women Who Need Donuts*. She is now sixteen. It's a whole new world.

She is brilliant and kind, conscientious, wise, funny. And so are her friends. The irony is the insecurity they all feel. They are all gorgeous. Talented, amazing kids.

One day, while driving in Hawaii. Avery said, "One of my friends is anorexic, and my other friend is sending me her waist size and is bragging that she's shrinking and losing weight, and she's already so skinny!"

I was driving on the highway, and I suddenly felt like I wanted to pull over. I started freaking out. I felt like Avery had just told me she, or one of her friends, was about to put a needle in her arm and give heroin a try.

"Oh my God!" I said. "We need to intervene! This is urgent." The reality of what she was casually telling me put me into panic mode. "You guys are sixteen! You are perfect, you are gorgeous. Please God, *no*! Don't start this spiral into self-hatred now. What can I do?"

It hit me that I'd started the diet obsession around that age, and it had ruined my life until now. I'm just now recovering from diet madness and the quest to be skinny and perfect and acceptable, and I thought, *What can I do to stop these girls from sinking into the abyss of self-loathing?*

Well, I realized, I could only start with myself and my daughter. I could tell her friends that they are beautiful. But I had to start with myself and hope that would influence my daughter. I could stop the diet madness and find some self-love, or else my words to her would be hollow. I could say, "Avery, you are beautiful, you are perfect," but if I didn't believe the same thing about myself, what good would my words be?

I say to her (and to myself), "Your beauty is your heart."

That's all you can do: reinforce the concept of that beauty,

beauty that radiates from the soul, from a beautiful and faithful heart, from a heart that believes in herself, believes in a good life, believe in the love in her veins. I pray that these girls know that their power is in their love, their femininity, their connection to God. I hope the same thing for myself. I wish someone had taught me this. Better late than never. I wish only self-love for these girls.

# BEING FORTY-FIVE

A ND THEN THERE'S ME: forty-five next week. I have to believe the best is yet to come.

Hope is my oxygen. There is always that little voice that says it's all downhill from here. How sad.

At forty-five, I'm making the choice to believe. To believe that life still wants to surprise me, still wants to stoke me, still wants to tantalize me and delight me. That is my mantra: the best *is* yet to come. I have faith in a good life. My favorite thing.

My inner love fairy (a.k.a. my desires) says, "What do you love? Just do that." I haven't been listening. She's been patient. She's been trying to get my attention forever.

"Go toward what you love," she says. "It's OK. Taste the raspberries, smell the peonies, sip the Bordeaux, allow the sun on your face. Lie in the grass, frolic in the waves, gaze at the stars, make out with your boyfriend, laugh with your people, swing on the rope swing, feel the wind in your hair, absorb the glow of the fire, toast the s'mores, and dig your toes in the sand. Live."

She's been taking my shoulders and gently pushing me toward the things I desire. And I've been digging my heels in the ground.

"No," I say. I resist. *I'll be over here ... a little bit cold, a little bit hungry.*

And she keeps pushing me, flapping her little wispy wings. "This way," she says. "You're close. Pleasure wants you. It is dying for you to have it. It wants to run through you. Turn your switch on. Take what life gives you, then ask for *more*. Life wants you to have more than you even think you want. Let yourself be pulled to the sunset, with a glass of wine and a bowl of grapes. Don't fight joy anymore. You're getting warmer. It's OK."

And then I soften. Surrender, letting her push my body toward the warm heat of what I love. I am home.

It's OK to be happy.

Here are the rules of the love diet:

- Cut out guilt.
- Reduce self-doubt.
- Eliminate mistrust.
- Add extra amounts of joy.
- Stir in a touch of pleasure.
- Dollop with gobs of passion.
- Garnish with a few ounces of peace.
- Sprinkle with lots of flavor, loads of love.

Results are guaranteed.

Four months passed. I relapsed. John and I relapsed. I sunk back into a food panic.

I wasn't feeling good, physically or relationship-wise. Once again, I tumbled into a quagmire of food obsession, thinking it was going to heal everything.

John and I had a good summer of boating. We had fun together, but we also had intermittent severe, heavy relationship drama. We didn't trust each other. We would spend time lovingly together, then hours later, he'd say, "I can't do this. And it's because of Hawaii. I don't trust you." Hours earlier, he'd trusted me. Then he switched his position. So I wasn't trusting him either.

I was devastated. I was spending so much time trying to prove

I was trustworthy, that I believed in our love, that I wouldn't hurt him, that our bond could endure. And it *did not work.*

Our love was rocky at best. I wanted to believe in forgiveness, and growth, and new beginnings. But it kept crashing.

I backed off. He said he needed time and "space." And I floundered. I wanted love—lots of it. I felt I had a lot to give. I had tons of love to give, and I needed a place for this love. I felt like I could see the healing. I felt like I could let go of the past and focus on the present, and the fact that I felt pure love. I wanted intensely to believe that love heals all.

I watched my food issues spiral. The correlation seemed apparent: love is hungry. I was so hungry for love. Yet I was dieting. I was trying to fix my broken heart through a diet. Turns out a diet can't heal your heart.

How many times do I need to remind myself of this? It's not about food, it's about my heart. It's about having what I want. It's about having it all. It's about living a life that I'm psyched about, that's full of passion, satisfaction, self-acceptance, and reality acceptance. It's about pleasure and allowing and giving my body what it wants—giving my heart what it wants, which is flavor and permission and abandon and green lights and yeses and freedom and pleasure.

I wanted to say yes to life and yes to love, yet I spent months dieting when John and I were rocky. I was trying to cure everything. I was torturing myself to heal my pain. I was in pain that John and I were falling apart, and I crucified myself. Pain and torture don't heal anything. Suffering doesn't cure shit.

Love is hungry. My heart was hungry. It was starving. I know it always has been. I've always had a sensitive, fragile heart. I watched my parents both try so hard at life and never really sink into a great romance with each other. Suddenly, John was not available to me, and I had to look at my hungry heart. It was like a romance novel/mystery to solve, and there was no resolution. It sucked. The despair was palpable.

I wasn't ready to accept a totally broken heart. I fought it like a bull. My deepest fear in life is realizing that sometimes things just bottom out. Life throws you curveballs. The love you want isn't always what's going to happen. The person you think is your person might not be your person. Heartbreak is just a part of the deal. Trust life? Have faith? Okay, I guess. Sure. But it sucks. I guess the heart makes mistakes sometimes. I had to mourn the disappointment.

I was hungry and am hungry all the time. I am hungry for love and life and food and satisfaction and contentment and affection and flavor and indulgence and all of it.

I knew there was a correlation between my love life and my diet. *Satisfy me*, I felt. *This being needs to be satisfied.* The beast was starving, my heart was starving, and yet I starved myself. I held back. I deprived myself of love, food, pleasure, fulfillment, happiness, satisfaction.

It wasn't John's fault. I restricted myself. I always had. *Let there be love, honey, let there be love.* I tried to convince myself that I was deserving, but love takes practice, and trust takes practice.

I realized that I was not being loving with myself. A constant diet is not loving; it's punishment. And so the pleasure log, the practice of eating whatever I wanted and whatever I craved, came back into play. Four months later, it came back into play. I had to build trust ... with myself! If I wanted to have trust and love in a relationship, I had to have trust and love with myself.

Food is my portal. It is my tool to gauge my self-love, my self-acceptance, my self-trust, my *I can love my life* tool. If I can't be trusted with my own desires, appetite, cravings, and the basic concept of feeding myself, how can I be trusted with someone else's heart? I am starting to take this very seriously. I eat whatever the fuck I want and watch how it helps to keep my heart open. A diet is like a padlock on the heart and soul. I can't simultaneously padlock my heart, appetite. and cravings and also pray for a good love life. Claudia Welch, author of *Balance Your Hormones, Balance Your Life*, says "Healing begins when we start to live the life we really want to be living."

I felt like shit. My body was still bloated; I couldn't drop the pounds I was carrying. I was desperate to feel better in my body. I was embarrassed and tired and obsessed with fixing myself with food. Diets, restriction, fasting, everything—nothing worked. I wanted John to find me attractive. I wanted to find myself attractive, and I felt gross.

My doctor said, "Your blood sugar is a mess. Your adrenals are a mess. Relax. And fix your diet." Ugh ... *fix* something, again.

Three years ago, I gained a bunch of weight, and my digestion was a disaster. I was bloated and sluggish and felt like hell. I couldn't digest life! My body reacted to my loss of hope, and this was my chance to restore hope. Hope equals healing; I see that now. I bottomed out a few years ago when my dad was dying, Donald Trump became president, my daughter was struggling with life, and I didn't see a light at the end of the tunnel. My body reacted. I could not digest life.

I want to live full-out. Louise Hay says blood sugar issues are an inability to accept the sweetness of life. Yes. That's me! I make donuts—I sell sweetness—but I couldn't eat them for years. I couldn't let myself have the pleasure. Now I acknowledge that I want to eat it up (life), devour it, indulge, live, cuddle up with someone, love them and love myself, let them love me full-tilt, let myself have cake. And a mocha. And life. All of fucking life.

I think I've always found some perverse honor in denying

myself. Forever. Like, "Hold back, have control, show some restraint. Don't be a glutton. Having it all is too much. Don't be too much." But I *want* to be too much. I am too much! Too much heart, too much appetite, too much energy, too much love, too much passion. I am quite simply way too much, and I'm not sorry anymore. God put this passion in me, and it's my duty to express it and satisfy it. I can't contain it anymore or I'll burst.

I've been naturally inclined to keep myself in a box. I have been a restrictor, but life has planted this longing in me to unleash the woman who wants it all and won't stop until she gets it. Love, abundance, pleasure, success, joy—fuck it, I'm not strangulating myself anymore. Life wants me to want and to have and to be way over the top in desire and expression and receiving. Life is begging to run through me.

Honoring our cravings is the highest praise of God. This makes me happy.

I wanted to heal through food, but I need to heal through life. I need to live the life I dream of, eat the food that I dream of, love the way I dream of, be touched the way I dream of—without games, without doubt, without holding back or restriction or dieting or mind-fucking. I can't diet and love at the same time. Dieting chokes my love. It crimps the hose, it stops the flow, it shuts down my heart. This woman needs to be a love line, giving love in all directions, to myself, to others around me, to my man. That is why I came to this planet—to love. I came here for love.

When I was seven, in second grade, I watched an after-school special. A little boy and a little girl fell in love, and then something happened. Their love didn't work out. They were neighbors, and one of them moved away or something happened to interrupt their love. It was so sad to me.

I remember being wholly devastated. I remember lining up with my second-grade class in the hall and feeling the whole day crippled with sadness—at seven years old. I moped through my school day just wanting to cry about these fictional characters who lost their love.

I hadn't thought about this memory in a long time until recently, I remembered the sadness. I think on that long-ago day, I realized having an open heart is incapacitating. I guess I decided that day I couldn't live like that, so sensitive and open-hearted. I couldn't feel what I felt so deeply and still function in the world. So I think that day, I started to turn my heart off, for survival, to be normal and not be so *weak*.

I lost the real me at age seven. I am a girl who just wants to love and be real about it. That's who I want to become again.

Less than two years ago, I took a dream trip to New Zealand with my daughter and my niece. I deliberately took them because all three of us needed hope, and I had an intuition that I would find loads of hope there (we did). I hired a tour company to show us the wonders of the North Island. It was pure magic.

The tour guides carted us around in a van and showed us the most incredible experience, with jaw-dropping views at every turn. Day one was a six-hour hike up a mountain. Every inch of New Zealand is bursting with green lushness, turquoise water, kind people, environmental awareness, and overall positivity. The hike was jaw-dropping.

Day two, we mountain-biked through redwoods and went white-water rafting, then jumped off cliffs and saw waterfalls that were powerful and mesmerizing. Day three, we went to the most glorious hot springs and floated in pristine, glistening natural baths. Day four, we explored Maori historic sites and witnessed hot geysers. The Earth and humanity seemed so interesting and fascinating and stunning. And I was sore. My legs were slaughtered still from the six-hour hike on day one!

On day four, I literally could not walk. Day five was slated to be the grand finale of this adventure tour that we had paid so much for. It was the last hurrah: a twelve-mile mountain crossing that people say is one of the most beautiful and scenic hikes on the planet. I'm not a hiker, and I was scared. And I still felt overweight and not at all fit.

I was intimidated to tackle this challenge. And my legs were absolutely killing me. At our dinner on day four, I made an announcement: "I can't do the hike tomorrow. I'm devastated. I can't walk. I can't even walk from this chair across the room. I don't know what's going on, but my legs are not recovered from that first hike on day one. Every step is excruciating, and I can barely even hobble. Every cell of my mind wants to do this hike, but it's not possible."

I was deflated. I literally thought, *If I can't walk across this room at nine o'clock at night without wincing in pain, how am I going to do a twelve-mile mountain crossing?* It felt surreal. I'd traveled across the world to see the wonders of New Zealand, and I had to bow out of the final adventure. I left the group and went to bed.

The next morning, I woke up at around five o'clock. (Way too early. I was exhausted.) I couldn't sleep, and I looked at my phone. It was February 14. Valentine's Day. I'd had no idea. I'd totally lost track of days in the Southern Hemisphere, as we were a day off from the United States. I think I thought that Valentine's Day was still a day away.

I felt a surge of energy from my dad. I got out of bed, and my legs were fine. The pain was gone. I thought, *Is this some sort of love message/miracle?* I got the overwhelming feeling that it was going to be a big day.

I looked for my sneakers. They were missing. I panicked. *I am not missing this hike! I'll have to do it barefoot.*

I ran to my niece's room and said to Cam, her boyfriend who was also with us, "I need your extra sneakers!" They were three sizes too big for me, but I threw them on, and I got on the bus. I felt cosmically that this hike needed to happen for something big for me. It felt like a conquest in my life that could be a life-changer.

Valentine's Day. My sneakers were huge, but my legs were functional. It felt like a test and a mission.

We headed to the mountain, and the guides scared us and prepped us a bit. They said, "There is no water for the next ten hours. So whatever you have in your bag has to last."

I felt really nervous. And then we all started marching. The sneakers felt ridiculous. We had about ten hours ahead, and I knew nothing about what to expect with the incline, the hiking, the terrain, any of it. I put one foot in front of the other, and it was hot as hell. There was no shade, and it was dry.

Our tour group was spread out. Avery was ahead of me. I soldiered forward alone, and I started to think, *It's time to love myself. Today is Valentine's Day, and it's time to love myself, and I have no idea what that means.*

I'd always thought I knew what it meant: love yourself, as in accept yourself, but in a superficial way. *Accept your thighs; accept your body.* But I hadn't questioned further the deeper concept of self-love.

I marched. There were a million stairs climbing straight up this mountain. The views in every direction were mesmerizing. And I was alone in my march. I could think of nothing else except self-love. I thought, *Today, I am going to find a strength that I didn't know I had. I feel heavy in my body. I feel insecure about my weight. I feel terrified of continuing to climb stairs in this heat for several more hours. My legs are burning from the endless climbing up the stairs, but my legs are functioning. I feel unsure that I can do it, but there is a force with me.*

That force was my dad. It was undeniable. It was his Valentine's gift to me: the encouragement to remind me of what I'm capable of. And I repeated, *It's time to love myself, and I don't know what that means.* It wasn't about my weight. It wasn't about how I looked. It wasn't about what I'd accomplished in life. It was about my God-self.

My lovability is my God-self, the me that's not my own. It's the God in me that loves humanity, the God in me that wants others to feel hope, the God in me that wants others to have a wonderful experience on this planet, the God in me who loves this Earth and is completely and utterly fascinated by it and appreciative of it, the God in me that loves. I have to get clear on this.

Today was the day. I marched in silence. I repeated and acknowledged that I would find my God-self, and I would love her. We teetered along a few really nerve-wracking edges of mountain. We slid down a pebble-covered decline where we could not get solid footing for an hour. It felt like quicksand. We stopped at so many vistas and saw old volcano tops blown off and then turquoise lakes that glowed in some otherworldly way. We were looking out and across New Zealand at completely majestic and ridiculously beautiful views.

Then we wound around paths covered in bright flowers and fragrant bushes I'd never seen back home. We finished in the shade, traipsing through redwoods that finally cooled us down the last hour after so many hours in the blazing sun. I was so incredibly thirsty, as my two water bottles were completely inadequate to manage the thirst of hiking twelve miles in the scorching sun. But we crawled to the end, and our tour guides had a cooler of beer waiting for us. It was the most glorious treat I'd ever had in my life.

I had a cold beer on a bench after the hot ten-hour challenge, and I toasted to my dad. He was a beer guy. Everyone knew that. He had two Miller Lites every night of his life.

The twelve miles was easier for me than I ever could have imagined. I sat at the finish, so hot and dirty and profoundly thirsty, and I thought, *Holy shit, I can do anything.* That day, I was fueled by love.

This year, I started a cookie business. I've moved on from donuts to cookies, and I'm starting the retail part of the business today. I'm getting keys to my new space. I am opening a boutique/gallery (my dream!) with art, music, cookies, coffee, wine, chocolate, and even intimacy oil—all my favorite stuff.

John will help me a little. Right now, we are friends. I still love him, but we haven't figured out how to heal and move on from all our challenges. So we are friends, and I'm sure he'll help me here and there with projects, starting with a sculpture for my gallery.

I love his art. I love his creativity. I am following my philosophy of running a business out of pure love. I did it before with donuts, but this is next level. It's *everything* I love: chocolate, wine, coffee, art, music—the sweet things in life. It is called the Wave. It's a wave of hope, a wave of things I love, a wave of purpose (part of the proceeds will go toward cleaner ocean efforts).

It's the wave of how I believe a business should be conceived: in love, in surrounding oneself in one's pleasures, and in self-belief. Pleasure heals. Joy heals. Hope heals.

I love this place already. I walk in and I feel like I do about the Holy Donut. I'm in love with it, like being in love with a person. If this doesn't heal me, I don't know what will. It's my final effort.

My body still doesn't feel like the old me, but I am betting on this storefront bringing me great health and contentment. I had been looking for health (and hope!) in dieting and in a man. Now I am looking for health and hope in permission—permission to eat, permission to start a business totally solo, and permission to be satisfied. I was looking for hope in a diet (*I'll be fixed! I'll be attractive and more lovable!*). Now I'm going to find hope in my morning mocha, baths, solitude, hard work, delicious dinners that I cook, and long walks.

I am crawling out of a hole of eating disorder hell. It's a practice, three times a day! Breakfast, lunch, and dinner are opportunities to eat with love, to live with love, and to be in love. *Love is patient, love is kind, blah, blah, blah.* Actually, love takes work sometimes. Self-love takes work. It's a daily grind for some reason. Accepting ourselves and our human quirks with open arms is a mission of love.

I am doing this for me. I really tried to heal myself through diet and fixing a broken relationship, and neither worked. So I'm sinking my heart and soul into this business. It is me. I am selling myself. Everything in the store is my passion. I realized whatever dream and cravings God placed in you (chocolate! music! wine! all of it!) is your lottery ticket. Your desires are your straight shot to success and money.

Your heart is your money.

Your heart is your money.

I'm going to surround myself with things I love. I am going to spend every day creating things I love and selling them. I have people making custom soaps, lotions, candles, art—all things

I've cocreated with these artisans. I stand behind everything I sell because I love everything in my store. The money is going toward cleaner oceans, another thing that I love.

I thought John was the love of my life. I've decided the love of my life needs to be *my* life. The love of my life *is* my life.

The best truffles, the best T-shirts, the best songs on the piano, the best organic coffee, the best wine. This is my dream. What you love will love you back, right?

John and I will love each other from a distance, from an independent place. I have let go. The best part of being single is I can let go of the obsession with looking better, being better. I can eat for me, live for me. Who was I living for? Who am I living for? **Who am I living for?**

I accept the heartbreak. People come into our lives for a sacred purpose. Sometimes they stay; sometimes they go. This six months of letting go has brought me closer to myself. I had to find myself as a single woman, a businesswoman, a woman who can go rent a space and start a business alone and find love, romance, and passion in her own daily life.

> Your daily life is your temple and religion, when
> you enter into it, take with you your all.
> —Kahlil Gibran

I am going to invest in myself. I am putting so much time and money into this. I am risking it all for love—this time for me.

I don't know what will become of my relationship with John. We will probably remain just friends. I knew I needed to find my God-self in New Zealand. At least I found her.

I trust life. I trust God, and I certainly do trust love, however it wants to be in my life. I trust love will guide me in this new business, and it will pay the bills. Love does the trick. A diet (vegan, fruit, no fruit, paleo!) didn't cure my heart. Building myself a life and business I love is my only option. It's the love diet.

Printed in the United States
By Bookmasters